FORGOTTEN COFFEE

Forgotten Coffee

Poems
by
ANDREA CLADIS

Adelaide Books
New York / Lisbon
2019

FORGOTTEN COFFEE
Poems
By Andrea Cladis

Copyright © by Andrea Cladis
Cover design © 2019 Adelaide Books
Cover image by David Hrivnak

Published by Adelaide Books, New York / Lisbon
adelaidebooks.org

Editor-in-Chief
Stevan V. Nikolic

All rights reserved. No part of this book may be reproduced in any manner whatsoever without written permission from the author except in the case of brief quotations embodied in critical articles and reviews.

For any information, please address Adelaide Books
at info@adelaidebooks.org
or write to:
Adelaide Books
244 Fifth Ave. Suite D27
New York, NY, 10001

ISBN-10: 1-949180-96-4
ISBN-13: 978-1-949180-96-1

Printed in the United States of America

Contents

Preface   *9*

Forgotten Coffee   *11*

PART I: BREAKFAST BLEND
"I Wanted To Find The Green Light"   *19*

When The Day Woke Up   *21*

The Dancer   *23*

Santa Monica Beach   *25*

7:00 Am.   *27*

Unlearned Lessons   *29*

Held For Decay   *35*

Weighted Walls, White And Weary   *36*

To Bed At Four, Up At Six   *39*

GROCERY, gratis.   *41*

Red Prius   *45*

Refugee Of America   *46*

PART II: ESPRESSO
"Awaiting the serenity"   *49*

Pandemonium   *51*

Green Fellow   *53*

Autumn Opossums   *54*

Happiness Is Time With Kody   *57*

The Chase   *58*

Glitter Bud Snowflakes   *60*

Even The Fish Needed My Attention   *61*

Home   *63*

Imperfect Symmetry, Unparalleled Destiny   *65*

On Running   *66*

Petros Thē Pelekános (πελεκάνος)   *69*

Wait. Walk. Run. Bleed.   *72*

PART III: MACCHIATO
"Time evaporates as the birds sing"   *75*

Water Conversations Bubble   *77*

The Chipmunk   *79*

Communion   *80*

Tears Stain My Suffocating Heart   *82*

An Apparition Of The Human Condition   *84*

Amnesia Asks The Question   *86*

Tethered By Time   *90*

FORGOTTEN COFFEE

Secrets Of Sleep   *93*

Holy Art Thou Underwear   *95*

Remorse, Victim Of   *96*

Beach Today   *98*

Return To Self   *99*

PART IV: FRENCH PRESS
"Longing for one last kiss!"   *103*

Hear Me, Just This Moment   *105*

Ruby Heart   *108*

Singing His Prayer   *109*

April Robin   *112*

The Mother. The Matriarch. My Yia-Yia.   *114*

Love Lingers In Longing   *119*

The Prince   *121*

Never Just A Kiss   *122*

To Know An Angel   *124*

Another Funeral   *126*

Unsalted Love   *128*

Farewell   *131*

About About the Author   *135*

Acknowledgments   *137*

Preface

Forgotten Coffee is a poetry collection that explores the human spectrum of emotion through examining the compulsions of living in an unpredictable world. A tight lens is placed on the haunting nature of time, the continual balance of joy and grief, and the wrenching, yet rousing experience of lost love. *Forgotten Coffee* is complex in its scope with the inclusion of humorous poetic anecdotes alongside the magical notion of believing in and living with a healthy dose of whimsy. The ecstasy of love realized and analysis of peril that exists within the human condition provide breadth to this collection. While the coffee of life might be forgotten, the extended metaphor within this collection is that we must always honor who made the coffee, how we connect to it, and why its animating impulse enriches our lives. For it is oft the simple things of life that are the most responsible for activating our emotional, physical, and spiritual responses. The objects in the margins are the invisible catalysts of our collective perception.

Forgotten Coffee

"Coffee, please."
    "Decaf?"
"It's 9 AM, regular with cream."

Regular with cream.
One more cup prepared to scream
in her face as she asked me again.

"Coffee, please. Where's my coffee?"

Floating grounds she left behind.
Cold, untouched coffee.
Simmering requests
for another brew.

Daily the chime,
routinely by nine,
but again at one and three.

"Coffee, please."

Counting cups.
She never knew
how many.

"Where's my coffee?
    It never came.
    What are those
    shapes you draw that
    make my name?"

Cup #204. *Letters.*
They are letters. My name is Rachel.
Yours is Rose. They are letters.

"Numbers and letters.
My address at home:
    423W.
The coffee.
    Is on
        the porch."

The coffee is on the porch of
the house that she
can still see, but
    no one can find.

Daily the chime,
routinely by nine,
but again at one and three.
"Coffee, please."

My name is Rachel.
For seventeen years I have brought you
warm coffee.

The shoe factory
where she once worked
smelled of leather.

"And oak," she said.

Like the porch swing
he built and stained from

FORGOTTEN COFFEE

the bent trees
that lost
branches
in that storm of
    1928.
And then forgot how to grow them again.

"Where's my coffee?"
    It never came."
    She insisted. Always. The absence of its presence.

My presence was with *its* presence.
Rachel. Your caretaker. For seventeen
years. I have made your coffee.
"I met a man today who called himself, 'William.'
    Or Wes? He said he knew me. A tease.
    A pleasure!
    My lips tingled the happiest tingle when he said,
    "Good morning, Mary."
Cup #231. *Wesley. Your husband.*
Wesley is the name of your husband. You married in 1943.

"Wesley's a handsome name.
    But I wish he had called me Violet.
    Or –
Rose. Yes. No. Maybe. Mary?
Rose, Rose, Violet. Rose."

Here's your coffee.
It's Rose.
Wesley kissed you.
Do you remember?

"Coffee, please."
Do you remember? My name is Rachel.
His name is Wesley. Your name is Rose.

"The porch needs fresh paint. The
railing is like a drowsy friend.
Bill can do it. My fingers are tired.
  324W. The coffee is on
     the porch."

Cold, untouched coffee.

Daily the chime,
routinely by nine,
but again at one and three.

"Coffee, please."
The cream and sugar were empty.
Powdered crescents remained.
The stale, forgotten cookies
frowned at
me.

I always brought the coffee.

She was a schoolteacher
whom children adored.

She was a wife
for whom her husband loved.
She was a coffee drinking, confabulating friend
Who rarely sipped any more.

FORGOTTEN COFFEE

"Where's my coffee?
    It never came.
    Where's this husband,
    Who doesn't know my name?"

"There were mums
on the porch.
    Purple.
        Yellow.
            Orange.

He planted them in the fall when
Chilled air came and black cats guarded
the pumpkins on the porch.
Their leaves always so crisp they scratched my fingers."

Cup #259. *Autumn.*
Wesley planted the mums during autumn.

"Numbers and letters.
    Wesley. Autumn.
    Mary.
        Violet.
Rose. Rose.
Rose Leigh Calstead who lives at W423 Hillside Avenue.
The coffee is still on the front porch swing.
Fallen oak.
Abandoned branches.
That tree withered with worry.
It still can't sing.
The way Bill had promised."
His name is Wesley. Your name is Rose.
Please tell me you know I'm Rachel.

Cold, untouched coffee.
Simmering requests
of memory.

"Coffee, please!"
    "Decaf?"
"It's 9 AM! Regular with cream!
Regular. With cream.
"Coffee!
    Please!
    Regular with cream and
    crescent moons."

Don't stare at me.
I'm not to blame.
Can you, Rose, please recite my name?

The paint-chipped porch left habitual slivers in her
weary hands.

Every morning at 9 AM, I served her coffee.

The coffee that remains on
the porch of the house
she can still see,
but no one
can find.

"Coffee, please."

Coffee.
Please.

Wesley-Rose
Tree branches.

FORGOTTEN COFFEE

Teaching. Children.
Hillside Street.
Coffee. Please.
Married. 324W. Avenue. Hillside.
Three uneven steps
the gentlest wind could disturb
Creaking ceaselessly.

A porch swing, barren white railing.
Rocking chair, unkempt cushion.
Wicker table, clouded glass top.

A ceramic rooster.
A threadbare Bible.
A stained mug of untouched coffee.

Daily the chime,
routinely at nine,
but again at one and three.

It's 9 AM and I only wish she knew me.
I only wish she knew me like she knew the
railing of her paint-chipped porch.

Cup #297. *Paint.* I painted the porch. *Again.*

I count 298 cups of coffee
and the first one is still
screaming its reminder –

Please.

I never forgot
The coffee.

PART I: BREAKFAST BLEND
"I Wanted To Find The Green Light"

When The Day Woke Up

When the day woke
I saw a rogue cloud cast its shadow on
     the lake's reflection.
The cloud, not quite covering the sun,
     flattened the moving water and
     turned the sky hazy.

I was praying for rain –
For a long, steady storm.

But the day woke up, opened its lungs,
pushed back the cloud
     The hovercraft on the lake, removed.
The lake,
     glistened.
The sun,
     shined.

My dog, caramel and white
     Wagged his shaggy butterscotch tail
     His body wriggled,
     Smiling at

The Sun.

I watched as new clouds threatened
     Swirling up confusion
As the day woke.

Andrea Cladis

The morning yawned and stretched.
Extended its hands through rays of quivering sunlight.
The lake breathed in wind-fueled currents.

The day gaining strength
    To lift the storm-dreamers from their beds,
    To invite the pallid skin-wanderers to be
        Warmed in Earth love.
When the day woke up it brought me with it.

The Dancer

The dancer as two
leads and follows.

The human vessel dares
breath exhales in falling action.
wonder meets
moments in motion.

Metallic walls cast reflections
multiplying gentle limbs
Parts as one,
flowing.

A visible silhouette, leotard of black
Lengthened legs float with ease
Filtered light casts shadows
adding dimension to the
body questioning the song.

The floor delicately worn by blistered feet,
the endurance of art.

Swimming on land the body remains open
Full extension, reaching as the child toward a mother.
Not knowing if the return touch will favor or falter.

The body is long, limber
        lean and learned.

Andrea Cladis

The body is strong, stirred
    The dance pauses,
        the body is turned.

Fluid and rhythmic,

This body -

    is beauty.

Santa Monica Beach

I will never forget
the luxuriant day we met.
Flowers of paradise, fluted glasses,
flirty Moscato wine.

You, an army pilot.
Me, a dancer.
We were barely 23.

Santa Monica beach was where you
first put your hand in mine.
Your warmth whelmed me.

The sun cast away shadows fromyour kind, handsome face.

You returned the fourth week of
every month.
Your dark eyes drew me in,
gentle hands excited my skin.

My pleated blouses, your tan corduroy
The dancer, the pilot,
One day to marry, have children -
One girl, one boy.

Last week, a vacant beach.
The sergeant said they
couldn't locate your
plane.

Andrea Cladis

Memories masqueraded.
Pain strapped my chest.
a whisper heard, but no one around.

Uncertainty the lone, vital sign
Our love stolen by the
innocent sky.

7:00 Am.

Sound is sorry silence.
Time lurches past his
empty, chalk-dusted chair.

He is an absent memory
released only by
aching want.

Unkempt linens
refuse to catch
stale cookie crumbs.

Untouched cereal
sugars the milk
in my breakfast bowl.

Boiling water spills
blistering my toes.
Ice tames my twitching thumbs.

Our wooden spoon
splinters my soggy hands
without appetite.

His unopened mail
feathers my briefcase.
Snickering at my
agitated hands

clutching the
sneering
spoon.

Spoiled peaches permeate
the back wall of my muted throat
softening the hollow air,
devoid of oxygen.

I envy their
Decay.

Unlearned Lessons

AUGUST OF EXCITEMENT

My freshman year at Francis Prep,
an all-girls Catholic school,
My English teacher
let students call her Anna, but
the head nun, Sister Mary, insisted we call her,
Miss Raditch.

*It was against the rules to call an adult by
their first name.*

If the school was like the cousin to religion,
Miss Raditch
was like the
tempting step-mom.

She had curly brown hair
and the most stylish shoes I had ever seen.
Her eyes would dazzle in theses sparkling
purple and pink hues of shadows and eyeliners until
Sister Mary made her stop wearing make-up.

SEPTEMBER OF LEARNING

Miss Raditch employed witty stories to
help our learning,
she brought a playwright named

Shakespeare into our classroom.
We learned about drama and tragedy.

She taught us five new words a day and told us
to use our imaginations.

My classmates and I
became good at writing stories
and discussing literature.

Lord of the Flies and *King Lear*
    The Sun Also Rises and
        The Great Gatsby.
I wanted to find the green light.
I wanted to scold Daisy for breaking Jay's heart.
It was against the rules to read about moneyed women,
Anna applauded my disdain for that flighty female.

OCTOBER OF WITNESSING

Sister came into our classroom every day to
watch Miss Raditch.

Sister took down the colorful
posters in our classroom.
The ones with cute animals and writing tips.
The ones with happy quotes to motivate,
To strive for excellence.

She stripped the walls of the poetry we wrote and
she broke the glass-front of the frames that held photos of
Miss Raditch's boyfriend, her dog, her grandma, her family.

*It was against the rules for a young teacher to
share her personal life with students.*

Sister made Miss Raditch buy new shoes
and wrap her hair in a bun.
She ripped out the pages of "King Lear"
and put them through a paper
shredder in front of our entire class on a Friday afternoon,
the day before Halloween.

"Trick or Treat," she said.
"Be thankful I'm protecting you from this evil."

It was against the rules to read plays and fiction.

NOVEMBER OF HEARING

One day, Sister Mary heard Miss Raditch
pray to Jesus and not to Mary and

she slapped her straight across the face.
Miss Raditch did not move, nor did she cry.
She taught us about forgiveness that afternoon.

My parents did not believe me when I told of this story.
The nun hit my teacher!

Enraged, we heard Sister
       call Anna a *little cunt* as we waited outside of her office.
            You piece of shit, Sister yelled.

Sister Mary was mad we learned from texts outside the Bible

She did not like the joy we found in knowledge.
Cloaked in that hood of holy black,
Sister Mary told us she prayed
our "Anna" would slowly sink towards
      Hell.

Wasn't it against the rules to pray for someone to go to hell?
Miss Raditch became cautiously reserved.
She read Bible verses in robotic tones.
She stopped sharing jokes
and she stopped teaching us words.

The stark walls made her colorful warmth cold.

We were no longer allowed to journal in class.
The word "imagination" was banned as was the word,

"metacognition."

To "think" too much was to invite inquiry.
Good Catholic girls were *not* to do that.

Yes, it was against the rules to think that
which had not already been thought.

DECEMBER OF PRAYING

Like an IV drip, gradual doses as
    worthless, pathetic scum,

made Miss Raditch thin.

FORGOTTEN COFFEE

Her smile withered into her loose clothing,
hair pulled back tightly,
removing the smile crinkles near her eyes.

A few weeks before Christmas Miss Raditch showed us
a video she made about our worth as women of
Christ.

We talked about how the symbolism in the video
related to the social commentary in
"The Taming of the Shrew."

It was against the rules to connect faith
to literature outside of the Bible.

The week before Christmas,
we found her keys on her barren desk.
She left us a kind note telling us to keep
questioning the world outside of pleated
skirts and biased books.

She told us to keep reading and creating.
She had laminated our crinkled poems that Sister
had torn from the walls and thrown in the
dumpster because that's where
"words" belonged.

SEMESTER GRADE: INCOMPLETE

Anna left us with sheets of the glittery stickers
she kept hidden in her backpack.

In solidarity, we all wore a sticker on
our right cheek every Friday
in honor of
our *real* sister.
We were glad to take a detention on her behalf.

Miss Raditch was against all the rules and that's why

I stopped attending that holy school
once the year was through.
I kept my poem and I wear purple eyeshadow that reminds
me to think and to imagine all that is yet to be.

I think I learned my lesson,
but regrettably we

never got to learn the rest of hers.

Held For Decay

Watchful walls trap the learner for four years' time.
Wide-eyed they enter, eager for the promise of fun.
Every hour a ringing bell pilfers their privileged prime.

A rupture of unfiltered frenzy and disordered lines.
Teachers smile as naiveté leans towards
the window warping the sun.
Watchful walls trap the learner for four years' time.

Assessments, grades, forced order
yields submission by design.
Tarnished trophies of unknown sports
icons stand for achievements won.
Every hour a ringing bell pilfers their privileged prime.

Complacent cattle feed; the freshmen, they climb.
Laughter casts its phony plea where the worn renegades run.
Watchful walls trap the learner for four years' time.

Imprisoned learners toil as obedient mimes.
While walls close in on the cry, "Are we ever done?"
Every hour a ringing bell pilfers their privileged prime.

Aching bodies of decay at graduation
once deemed sublime.
Numbed as perfected antiseptic
products, each and every one.
Watchful walls trap the learner for four years' time.
Every hour a ringing bell pilfers their privileged prime.

Weighted Walls, White And Weary

Racked weights.
Empty Benches.
Hungry Solitude.

Shadows silhouette the waiting corner bench
Flickering light, the halogen halo,
Irritates.

The walls see all weakness,
     absorb all want.

Stable body.
Secure frame.
Braced core.
Just one set more.

Run.
Lift.
Rush.
Swell.
Repeat.

Hours staring
at the white wall,
lifting.
The mirror,
mocking.

FORGOTTEN COFFEE

A reflection.
An obsession.
The narcissist's sin.
Vanity, says the cinder block wall,
Is captured within.

Aim for speed
The force of sinewy strength.

The walls see me tremble,
    fear my failure.

Four corners.
Two stops.
Ropes and hurls.
5 burpees.
10 jacks.
Stripped resistance curls.

White walls.
Brandished thoughts.

In competition -
Self is first and
Ego, destiny.

Sweat trickles.
Pain pleads.
A wish for
new strength.

Outside,

the world smiles,
 laughs, indulges,

　　　Effortlessly.

Inside, the metal cylinders
 work, perspire, and listen

　　　Cautiously.

The walls restrict.
White and watching.
Wanting and winning.

Lifting up, down, right, then left
Compulsion.

The walls touch my back.
The walls hear my breath.
The walls don't know my name.

Vainglorious,
This giant's game.

To Bed At Four, Up At Six

Dad woke me up at 6 AM.
"Morning, kid! Time to clear some snow!"

Hats, jackets, mittens cover sleepwear
Snow sticks to eyelashes, red shovel in hand,
my well-rehearsed legs traveled the

long driveway where
I watched Dad's struggle –
man's worth versus the snow blower
hood, coat, hunched over, his frosty breath
between his shoulders.

Lift, push, lift, pull, release the crank
a breath in, a breath out.
A whimpering machine chortles creating

swirling snow.
We tame the boss of winter.

A new snowdrift growing from the west
Eyes meet in the sparkling flecks, a path almost cleared
a snow truck
interrupts our
progress.

Andrea Cladis

The doctor goes to bed at 4 AM, and must get up at 6,
a dad, a daughter,
work in tandem.

Sleep waits, dawn fades.
Snow blankets our time together.

A once boastful machine sputters, red shovel rests,
a snowclad neighbor raises his arm, a solitary toast.

To bed at four, up at six,
A father's pride.

To bed at four, up at six,
Each snowflake tickles
our bond.

GROCERY, gratis.

I waltz the labeled aisles
listening to
classic music.
Melodious the repeat
The sounds and smells.

My green plastic cart
lacks direction.
It wriggles.
The pesky black wheels
refuse forward motion.
Swerving slowly
I hum happily.

The quiet space
at the day's end
comforts me.

The bakery wants my business
A frosted heaven
of temptation.

I breathe in the aroma
reminiscent of my 16th birthday
and that delicate cake layered with strawberries
and custard lining the roof of my mouth.

The coffee tastes better only because it's free.
Unlimited samples,

Andrea Cladis

I act as a child -
adding cream and sugar beyond satisfaction.

Bulk food bins taunt,
I want some, but not all

Lights gently dim as
patrons filter in.
An elderly gentleman
rubs his hands carefully
over the soft red grapes and bruised kiwis.

Delicately filling his basket with those
cholesterol saving, doctor-approved armfuls of
greens, vitamins, prune juice, and low-sugar oatmeal.

He hunches until his back pauses and he can
set his basket down
while a young, pregnant mother asks
if the bruised kiwis taste better than the hard, fuzzy ones.

Sipping his coffee sample – black, no cream
The old man holding red grapes offers advice:
Eat only the fruit that has not been forced to ripen -
the fruit that was slow to ripen, but will
be thrown away tomorrow.

Staring at her pregnant belly the young woman explains
how she fears for the health of her child.
The gentleman reminds her, the child
must ripen as will the fruit.

FORGOTTEN COFFEE

Smiling they part ways,
the mother continuing
to encircle the store
craving foods she's never eaten before.

The elderly man now waiting to pay
watches a small boy sneaking candy from the endless
bins of sugared colors.

Chocolate, licorice, peanuts, and popcorn.
The boy is no scofflaw.
He's just a kid and for now his mother
is buying produce he knows he will have to eat later.

But at least he can't locate prunes or oatmeal in his cart.
Someday he will though. And the candy will be
too sweet for his teeth or
will irritate his tender gums.
And the brownies he hid underneath
the lettuce won't taste the same
Because chocolate will lose its flavor
and his doctor won't know why.

Scanning the aisles to no avail
a flustered husband tries to fulfill his wife's honey-do list
Up, down, right, then left,
the swollen shelves bemuse him.
What brand does she want?
Why do we buy these things?
This is too damn expensive.
Where's the salsa and chips?
The mashed potatoes, the fresh steak?

Andrea Cladis

What the heck in cornstarch used for?
Cumin…is a spice?
Lentils or legumes?
Where is my wife!!

And in tandem they work
For chore, for recreation, for sustenance
The old man, the soon-to-be mother, the mischievous boy,
The conflagrated husband.

They shop, they smile, they furrow their brows.
They sample fragrant coffees and salted treats.
And they stop for a moment just to think
How lucky they are to have money and
food at the ready for purchase.

Baskets, carts of food in tow.
Money to be spent before they go
The exit slip allows them to leave -
The receipt they hold says they can sit and eat.

Shelves being re-stocked in the open rooms
All those new foods yet to be consumed -
Candy, oatmeal, and even prunes!
Will be lost to empty stomachs tomorrow by noon.

Red Prius

A shiny Prius
Driven by a creepy clown
Plays charades with me.

Refugee Of America

Terminals full
Every flight overbooked
A storm chasing millions inland
Threatening ice, snow, wind -
Power outages, distance from family and friends
waiting on the other end of the canceled flights.

On my fifth flight and third layover
carrying dirty clothes and bags of books,
Fatigued from lonesome hours and loathing looks
from strangers at the airport saying,
> *This must be what it feels like to be a refugee.*

A French-Syrian refugee heard my plea –
Her fixed, hollowed eyes dove into me.

"Ah, oui! Bien sûr. *A refugee of America -*

> Where the money and the planes
> Clean water and new strangers
> Will take you anywhere it is safe and not complain.
> Where you're warm quand il est froid and cooled
> quand il est chaud.
> Where you have food to eat and dry socks on your feet
> Where you have phones and power
> Electricity and a shower
> Internet and opportunity to be seen as
> > *Human.*"

FORGOTTEN COFFEE

Où les gardes avec des fusils protègent l'homme et la femme
et même en danger la sécurité est proche.

"Oui, vous etes un *vrai* américain," she said observing
my winter jacket, wool scarf, waterproof boots.
My books proving literacy, my phone fawning affluence.
A fresh water bottle cradled in the
side pocket of my backpack.

"What an inconvenience it must be
pour un réfugié *américain*
     en Ameriqué.

Quelle Horreur," she said, her hissing eyes
retracting. "Quelle. Horreur."

PART II: ESPRESSO
"Awaiting the serenity"

Pandemonium

Tom Petty jams pulsing.
The autumn breeze coaxes away tears.
    There's stillness in the calm,
    There's wisdom in his song,
        "Runnin' Down a Dream."
We might not realize our fugacious fantasies.

Quotidian sounds erupt with the unmasked sun
Slender sunlight awakens my feckless face.

The neighborhood quidnunc rattling off a rant
Her bafflegab, boisterous, she can't stop to think.

That nudnik dog starts barking,
    The birds are chirping back -
The morning canine chorus and that
soprano duck who quacks.

I want to thropple those perky, power-
walking whippersnappers –
    If only those gossiping pink shoes actually made them
    walk faster.
    Plastic bodied blondes -

Behind me a red machine chortles –
    It puffs, it sneers, it grunts and snortles
        It finds a humming rhythm;
        Now, I'm smelling green -

Andrea Cladis

An earthy taste lines the back of my throat;
I swallow – the sensation is clean.

A crusted sandman peeled from the eye,
Here comes the catawampus clamjamfry.

A hum, a thought, a brouhaha –
A day is born again.
Much to know, more to see,
The rest? Just barmecide.

Green Fellow

I stopped to write along the trail
    when this happy fellow
    befriended me.
Covered by a smooth pastel green,
    he hopped to no avail.

As he wriggled slowly,
moving closer and closer to me,
    I giggled as his webbed feet suctioned snugly
        to my knee.

The gravel massaging his underbelly
    he really seemed to like,
And so I didn't have the heart to tell him
    I nearly crushed him with my bike.

Autumn Opossums

Slowing my car, I squinted at
the wide animal making its 5 AM passage.
Her movement halted;
Her eyes flashing like the glowing numbers on my dashboard
screaming my tardiness for work.

I was perpetually late for my 5:30 AM classes
Thirty women and three men were awaiting
their morning dosage of endorphin earning, sweat shedding,
calorie torching training.
They would not be pleased to wait.

I wanted to honk my car's horn,
like an impatient truck driver during evening rush hour.
I wanted to get out and clap my hands,
like a football coach after his team's raucous huddle.
But the ambient homes slept,
and the moon still shone.

She started moving, more slowly than before
and soon one became two, and two
became three, and three became
nine small children tucked up into her body,
hidden from the lights of my car,
awaiting her next move for safe passage.

The smallest ones latched onto her tail like mice,
the larger babies rode piggy back

FORGOTTEN COFFEE

clumsily pushing into her soft, bushy fur.
My irritation deflated at
their efforts to travel.

I used my car lights to illuminate their way.
From one side of the street to the other,
Then from alley to alley, and dumpster to dumpster.
Mom stopped in the parkway,
watching me as I drove forward again.

Noticing her wooly white hair upright in alarm,
Sipping on three-day-old coffee from a leaky thermos,
I stopped as another small opossum popped into the street
Lost from the pack that had crossed.
Mom's glowering eyes looked into me.
The abandoned opossum was making
me even tardier for work.
10 missed burpees, and five fewer lifts
to fulfill the Monday madness.

I flipped on my right blinker to direct him to his mother
The orange distraction uprooted him; he followed to reunite.
Along with his brothers and sisters,
Waiting aimlessly on the other side of the street.
Mom's eyes morphed into a soft gray as she
looked once more in my direction.

My car engine muted as I
turned off my lights,
inviting moon shadows
so she could scurry off with her children
past the sidewalk, safely to the underbrush.

Andrea Cladis

I drove off, the orange light a penetrating memory
blinking wonderment in my mind.

I envisioned daybreak for those posturing opossums.
Their will for survival renewed.

Perpetual is life in the darkness
Longing for security
Apart from the light of day.

Happiness Is Time With Kody

Face hidden in fluffy, caramelized hair
Snuggles for a blink until the clever tease begins –

Hidden treats and performance feats,
I ask, "Who is making the rules?"

We giggle; we chase
We snack; we yap
We play; we nap
Just making me laugh.

We are happy for this moment of spontaneous joy -
Two triumphant, tail-wagging friends –
Never to be content when playtime ends.

The Chase

She jumped.
      He bopped.
She rallied her bushy tail up the tree.
           He circled her like a dizzy fish
           caught in a wave.
Nature's roundabout.

If squirrels can't fly, that's a lie
From tree-top to tree-top

She jumped.
      He hopped.
Their bushy tails met.
Up and down the tree,
The ongoing spiral,
The chase.

She stopped at the top.
      He batted her head with
           playful claws.
      Hello, friend!
      He said.

Swiveling of ankle joints for better grip,
She ran headfirst.
      He followed.
Their love-struck agility,
A marvel.

FORGOTTEN COFFEE

She waited.
    He ran towards another tree.
She leapt after him.
    His front limbs patted the stubborn ground.

Pat, pat.   Pat, pat.
Pat, pat, pat.
Four feet in tandem.

She listened, her head to the ground.
    His tail cocked -
    an acorn.

She jumped.
    He dug up the treasure.
She flitted her eyes,
Showed off her curvy tail.
    He offered the meal he had
        saved.
    Hidden to stave off winter's
        hunger.

She wrapped her tantalizing tail around her
beauteous face.

Nature's romance thrives.
The best laid acorn is their only
means to survive.

Glitter Bud Snowflakes

Oh, last evening I stared into the sky
    as tiny little glitter buds danced into my eyes,
Tickling me tenderly for quite a while,
    my lips effortlessly stretched into a seamless smile.
Falling gently,
    Fast…
        then slow –
            Falling everywhere the winds did blow.
Speckled against a sky so gray,
    Floating crystals in a mesmerizing display.
        Surrounding me with warmth and light –
        I no longer felt the burden of the night.
      Delicate snowflakes melted on my cold, brown eyes
        Cloaking my body in pure white –
          A flawless disguise.

Even The Fish Needed My Attention

The dog needed a walk.
Bills needed to be paid.
My boss called again. My inbox was full.
The family needed dinner.
I had another class to teach.
Mom had cancer.
And even the fish needed my attention.

Sapphire blue painted his body
Crimson red veiled his fins.
Like a pinhole button,
Those poppy seed eyes
poked out at me
through the glass.

His fins lagged as
my shadow moved away
inviting light into his tank.
My heart submerged in the foggy water

Mom would have another surgery.
She wanted to decorate for Christmas.
Dad yelled. My brother scoffed.
My sister cried.

Mom had cancer.

Witnessing my return,

Andrea Cladis

Poseidon greeted me in a flurry,
his fins remained eager,
I promised to always feed him.

The fish didn't know Mom had cancer.
      He needed me, too.
The fish didn't know Mom had cancer.
              Or did he?

No one wants to swim alone.

Home

I wish to return to the place I call home –
the fellowship of its grace,
I wish to return to the home I know –
but not the one that occupies space.

As humans we crave belonging, the
pinnacle desire to be loved.
The earthly wants of human touch,
Augmenting the spirit we grasp above.

Loving is missing -
Longing.
Wanting.
Receiving.
Loving is smiling, its vision, living.

I want to return to the protective embrace –
The warmth of the man I adore.
The one who sees me barren-faced,
The man who's helped me soar.

My busy mind he quells with ease,
Laughter fuses hearts in time.
When darkness whelms, I'm on my knees,
In absence he senses I'm all but fine.

A forehead kiss, a wink on the nose,
Eyes of adulation, my spirit he sees.

Andrea Cladis

Sandy numbness, love tingles my toes,
His smile, my happiness he frees.

Awaiting the touch, I'm not alone
Awaiting the serenity –
Soul meets home.

Imperfect Symmetry, Unparalleled Destiny

Flying High.
Floating
Low.

Traveling A
where geometric
blissful pattern
summer delicately
winds caressing the
will cloudless
blow. sky.
Polychromic
radiance
dances
upon the
unassuming
eye.
Temptress
of Five
hope. markings
Spectacle of
of blue
allure. azure.
A journey, that's free.
A past, that's lost.

Unparalleled destiny.
Nature's colors will cross.

On Running

Steps eat away the uncharted distance.
The shadow of balmy breath expelled,
Heartbeat matched rhythmic stride.

Heels swell, gripping the earth,
propelling my body forward.

Sweat droplets dance in the crease of my left eye,
I blink, they fall,
salt to my lips
The pulse in my temples teases
my mind.

>My feet numb beneath me,
>My hands clammy.
>My legs continue to climb.

My knees buckle, I stay upright.
The repetitive tempo,
the tantalizing chill of the night breeze with
its surrounding halo of warmth.

Dusk falls.

Streetlights flicker
The blood orange sun slips behind the dense
Trees.

My breath slows.

FORGOTTEN COFFEE

Stealth silver boomerangs deflect light from
the side panels of my scruffy shoes
cars cruise,
mellow music hums,
fashioning the peerless complexion of a
late summer night.

Crickets tap dance between blades of grass
The ground winds amplify their recital
Lightning bugs flash, fearless in flight
My final paces lead me home.

My scraggly pony tail flops
Eyes close; lungs exhale.
A whisk of cold air whelms my shoulders
I slow my steps on the driveway,
send a prayer to the coming stars –

My dog wags his tail at me from his perch
    He tilts his head back, howls for my return.
        Fog from his breath clouds the window,
      I smile.

My face tingles.
Another exhale.

My heart depleted of oxygen works to recover.
My legs throb from hip to ankle,
weary, but satisfied.
My dog darts towards the door.
When I enter, he will lick away my sweat and whimper
willing away my absence.

I am loved. I matter.

Andrea Cladis

I'll hear Dad holler an offer of ice water;
Mom, her mouthful of political banter -
the foolish laws and
Illinois lobbyists who unionize
every industry.

For one final summer minute,
I find myself
captive to nature's clarity.
Arms outstretched, the untouchable sky.
The earth swollen with joy.
I remove the bands holding
my hair and the

    night whispers its untold secrets,

        only the runner knows.

Petros Thē Pelekános (πελεκάνος)

He glides amongst the pebbled sand
Ivory feathers, a rusty orange beak
The Mykonos shore is home to

the great bird of iconic lore.
Like the American tourists, I call him, "Pelican Pete."
My father, a native, reveres Petros pistós,
The loyal seabird who

ladles in his mouth
rations of fish for the
men and women of the isle who
saved his life in the great storm of 1954.

The fisherman who found him
wounded, unable to fly
nurtured him back to health.

Once Petros had wings
ready for new flight,
He decided to stay near
the people who helped him.

He would not migrate again.

Sifting rocky sand between my toes,
I wonder why

He has never left.
He could soar the Aegean or
fly to Crete.
But each day he dances and fishes

along the firth.
Beneath the undulating shadow,
The blue and white emblem
reminds of the

heritage, that he
is a part of.

My father told me to be more like Petros –

To be hospitable,
To stay near family,
To honor my past.

But I wanted to be more American
A fast-paced life, moneyed job,
City walls containing me.

We took a picture together,
Petros pistós, boldly present in
the background.

On my return home
I looked at a photo of
the Mykonos mascot.

I rubbed a tattered piece of the Greek flag I

had uncovered on the beach
between my thumb and index finger.

My American city didn't know the amity of
an ocean or
how to love a bird.

I wanted to be treasured and cared for
To learn the compassion in the
heart of the fisherman.

I was tired of flying away from the
shore.

Wait. Walk. Run. Bleed.

I wait for truth in the promise,
The men will return.
The war they are fighting is
    never over.

I wonder if they lose,
    do they come home alive?
If they win,
    do we count the bodies?

I walk towards a placid river bank.
I count two comforting, pearl clouds -
the sky in the river's reflection.
Stagnant water, the clouds hog the rain.

There's an otter covered in
sticky, Alaskan algae.
Nature's camo.

Does he know I can see him?

I walk towards a faceless sun.
I run from swelling fear
The men are not
    safe.

I wait for peace.
The falling sigh,

my breath,
distressed.

His belly up to the sky
I tell the otter
I do not understand their bravery.

We are floating.

The static space between
Ambiguity and reality.
His eyes close,
silken fur expands into the water.

He dives,
He swims.

Life goes this way.

I walk towards a tottering tree,
separated by a single stroke of lightning.

And I run until
the wound is cauterized.

In a forest, alone.
Silent songbirds pucker their feathers.

    The men are not
        home.

PART III: MACCHIATO
"Time evaporates as the birds sing"

Water Conversations Bubble

Neighbors confabulate, it's early June
Sunscreen zephyrs fog clean morning air.
Lungs suffused with chlorinated pools and freshly cut grass
Smooth, summer jazz plays recycled repeats.

Conversations about Maggie's dog
bubble at the water's surface
Brilliant sunlight pierces.
He only had three legs, but the mutt
was a terror.

Waves rush against youthful skin
Smiles lighten children's faces.

He tore up my yard, and Sally's,
and also our neighbor, Jerry's
Not once but three times last summer.
Maggie claimed it would not
happen again.

Faux palm trees wade in sandy water.
Summer makes winter's enemies, friends
Rafts cushion past conflict
Slides sweep everyone into the same pool.

Sally wanted money to plant new flowers,
Jerry offered to fertilize our lawns.
I gave Maggie a coupon to buy a fence.

Andrea Cladis

Lifeguards lather on lotion
Free from school, children carouse.
Neighbors jest about their pesky pets.

The skirmish will wait.
Chocolate ice cream cones melt away worry.

At the waters' edge we watch
the time float by.

Friendship is not a shallow pool.

The Chipmunk

Escaping mangled floras
onto the crushed gravel path he came
A lively fellow wriggled happily
towards misfortune again.

A round, rouge berry teased his beady eyes
Quickly he darted, but too late to realize -

His midday snack had been spoken for,
Consumed by a hungry, cleated tire.
The chipmunk lured by natural desire,
Was now to be no more.

Tail in spoke,
Tangled, he broke -
The berry stained the tire.

Furry remnants lay in wait,
The gravel path's anticipated bait.

For the next creature or critter at bay,
Treading ruins, the swift attack,
Prepares at once for its new prey -
A freshly fated snack.

Communion

Soggy, not sweet.
I did not want to eat his flesh.

I had been diminished by disease,
Seven years of unanswered prayer.

Dried crumbs on the counter.
Bread without salt won't rise.
The engraved chalice holds
warm wine with granulated bits of
His body.

I asked God why the sun he created caused cancer.
I asked God why I was chosen to suffer.

I soaked hopes in His red blood.
I indulged in His white body.
I was told loving Him would rescind the cancer.

The Priest with a long golden spoon
Forced down throats the proof of His sacrifice
The promise of His existence.

I was 35 and would leave behind three children,
My home, my wife,
my life still left to live.

Engorged white bread dripping
with wine.

FORGOTTEN COFFEE

Altar boys and cantors.
The incense gathered its false promise.

Chanting choir.
Communion was finished.

The cancer spread.

A sandpaper throat, it was only the wine I tasted.
God knows I will spit out the grainy remnants of
     His body.

Tears Stain My Suffocating Heart

Those tears come down,
They cover my face
And I cannot place
That tired, kept frown.

And though my heart aches
I long to feel the pain
Memories in my brain –
Swallow this twisted fate

[CHORUS]
For tears stain my suffocating heart
I'm here; stranded, wandering in the dark
For tears stain my suffocating heart
Drowning in this salted love; wounds burn, I'm torn apart.

My sight isn't clear,
All objects a-blur
I'm lost, insecure
Trapped by relentless fear

This love is gone
Emptiness here alone
No grace have I been shown
I wait for the dawn
[CHORUS]

A memory here today
Breeds hope for tomorrow

FORGOTTEN COFFEE

Yet cloaked by this sorrow
How long must it stay?

Silence is my walk
Those steps have left my side
In whom shall I abide?
I seek not to hear, to speak, to talk

[CHORUS]
I've lost a friend
Who was close to me
A soul's been set free -
Though this heart will never mend

But I can endure
I'll praise God above
The treasure of such love
In HIS plan I am sure

[CHORUS]

Repeat x 3 with fade out: 'For tears stain my suffocating heart…'

An Apparition Of
The Human Condition

I have not made a list of things in naught but seven days,
Time lost to question, a clock to forgo
Deadlines diminished, decayed on the worn rocks.
Urgency, but a silver shadow.

Salty air trims my neck,
A sublime mystical motion, the ocean's exhale.

There's transparency in this moment
Collapsing lungs, clean horizon
Warm hues, motile sound,
Exuberant equilibrium found.

I wonder what remains to see past sky
painted sails and endless sea,
A future swelled on a patient past –
Shipwrecked beaches, abandoned like a grifted cast.

We frame and we measure every success,
The low tide reveals I've failed the test.

Overweening pride raptures every man,
The quest to harness beauty –
A fallacy to think we can.

Alas! This vision by the seas seems to dismiss –
The confrontation,

FORGOTTEN COFFEE

our mortal loneliness.

Wholeness felt within the spectacle of natural beauty –
This temporary connection to the metaphysical brings pity.

The sun will rise and set, these words may dance on pages,
but here in brokenness lies a sad note unaged.

Lost I remain, this cruel capitulation –
the limited apparition of our human condition.

Amnesia Asks The Question

Are you aware of what was on the news?

My friends ask as if I must know,
I should know!
How dare I be so ignorant?
I tune in to the news.

Another shooting!
Government Shutdown!
Those damn Democrats!
Those useless Republicans!

                                         The world's on fire
                                         Everyone's fighting wars
                                         I inquire in desperation,

What are we even fighting for?

The news chimes, *We promise!*
The news repeats, *We swear!*
The news insists on immediacy,
    It's always do or die.

                        I am free in nothing.

The cycle, endless.
The TV flashes
    colors,

FORGOTTEN COFFEE

    words,
    images,
    art
The radio cacophony
        of belligerent talk show hosts
        aggravates my peaceful drive
        to work -
We interrupt your programming for
this "special" news brief.

       The digital propaganda clutters my mind.

Did you hear the news today?
Amnesia asks the question again.

        Bickering, taunting, frivolous chatter.
        What in the hell, does it even matter?

Are we entertained by death?
Are we ever amused by grief?
Are we so well-trained to keep everything unjust, brief?

Everything the same.
Every.
Thing.
The.
Same.
Enough to make
Everyone!
    Everyone!
Insane.

Andrea Cladis

        Terror
            Here!

        Comedy
            There!

    Science moves the world?

Why the need for shouting rants?
Why the repeated, useless chants?

                I'll think for you, they dare to say,
                  I know what it is you want.
                We are here to ignite your doubt!
                  We are here to fuel your rage!

Why am I still listening?

Yes, we are here to tell you how to think and
how to feel!
how to vote
and what to eat.

        Everything's *still* the same!
          The infinite refrain.

Wonder, wallop, fear, excite,
argue, coddle, stir the fight!

        Mornings at 4, 5, 7, and 10.
        Evening news at 4, 5, 7, and when?

FORGOTTEN COFFEE

My friend, Amnesia, asks,

Did you hear the news?

"No." I muted the radio.

That's enough for today.

Tethered By Time

I slink into the bathroom trailed by
my robe's shadow.

The mirror reveals gray hairs lining
up on the crown of my head.
The fading brunettes of a prime lost to
time as regret stares back
at
       Plummeting
              expectation.

Why, mirror, do you imitate my physical compunction?

In its reflection, the clock of 4:30 reads 8:30,
      or does it say half past seven?

The mirror is still judging me, but
I can't see the gaps of time I missed.
The time I spent as a teen in the hospital
refusing to eat,
wishing to die.

The sun on the cusp of the horizon says
it's morning.
The birds in their chambers of
ruffled feathers echo
their songs on the

FORGOTTEN COFFEE

telephone line,
the chirping of time

scares me.
How much do I have left?
My youth wasted seeking perfection.

The clock now at three.
The mirror perches it at nine.

The thumping in my chest grows
when the mirror mocks my soft whites and grays.

The creases in my forehead breathes
into the corners of my eyes
Where is the young girl
who once idolized her image in this mirror?
What contempt I have for the chore of living.

    The routine march of days has made me old.

Wake up with wrinkles.
Wake up with shock.
Wake up with a souvenir to say –
I never stopped the
clock.

Time evaporates as the birds
sing.

The mirror looks on and I ask for

Andrea Cladis

help to wash away the wrinkles
and comb away the grays,
to give me a second chance.

Tethered to the cadence
At four o'clock or eight
At three o'clock or nine.

Secrets Of Sleep

The only thing she could not stop was
    Time.

Slumber became her chosen state,
resting early and sleeping late.

Maternal moments relayed on repeat,
nullified pulsating pain she was fain to suspend.
Maternal moments saved from delete,
amplifying imagination, a mind to transcend.

    The curious child,
        the very best friend.

Lullabies and plump, powdered skin.
Cries for attention, to hold and to spin.
Maternal moments, mother and kin.

A daughter. A son.
Softly at play.
A sun. A sky.
Brightly the day.

Meadows so pleasant she smiled with her eyes -
Endless hills and placid prairies.
Maternal moments, those imperfectly perfect, soft memories.

In her mind she sensed their smooth hands

clasped inside hers,
squeezing tightly
in need and want.

In her mind she cared for them when irritants of illness came
Preening hair and caressing cold shoulders,
with only herself to blame.
Maternal moments, if only she could
give, a mother's magical touch.

In her mind, they were shopping for shiny things,
And at home they were making music that sings.

In her mind, cookie dough stuck together fingers and toes,
And sugared flour created rosy cheeks of snow.

In her mind,
Laughter.
    Crying.

Love –
    Undying.

A mind best kept in
the secrets of sleep
where enchantment never fails its dream.

Maternal moments, a riddled mind.
The only thing it could not stop was

    Time.

Holy Art Thou Underwear

A grand eruption.
      A Volcanic force.
A vibration so intense -

I trembled.

Gripping sheets,
Compelled to inflation
By fatal flatulence.

Parachute pants
His holy boxers

Can you believe, it's all one man?

I prayed into the building warmth,
     "Father! Thy will be done!"

Through the smoke cloud,
A gasp for clean air,
A glimmer of white!
I rolled over to kiss him and
That's why he made me his wife.

Remorse, Victim Of

I saw my mother's tears.
I heard my father's pleas.
I felt the plague of guilt.
I knew the lies I told.

cunning words like the blood seeping from my gums
that no one could see
only I could taste.

I knew the taste of Orbit Bubblemint
gum that would keep me
      from ingesting calories at lunch.
I felt uncomfortably complacent to the scale holding steady
      at 60 pounds.
I heard therapists denying my
      humanity.
I saw my glowering face,
      the crest of my cavernous collarbone.

I knew my father trusted my every word,
I felt every calorie expand in my stomach, my thighs
I heard arguments about my thin, bony shoulders
I saw the reflection of a sallow girl.

small, protrusive bones in my feet, easily bruised
crescendoing requests to eat
a Honeycrisp apple larger than my fist.
dying would mean freedom.

FORGOTTEN COFFEE

the constancy of cold
the scalding tea I couldn't swallow,
a mouth lined with cotton.
"What's the matter with you?"

I won control over my mother,
her demand for perfection.

clumps of curly brunette hair carpeted my bedroom floor
me trembling beneath the weight of self-hatred

mom fading into despair as a poinsettia
exposed to cold, winter air
would I ever be enough?

Whispers wishing to dissolve self.
Whispers wishing to perish into warmth.
Whispers wishing to

SCREAM. OUT. LOUD.

I listened. I believed in
the wishful whispers that told me to
carry on and complete the quest.

The faded whispers,
more muted now at distance,

I still hunger for their restless wish.

Beach Today

What I found on the beach today,
    It surely wasn't time.

I found on the beach today,
    Grew in my hand alive.

    Found on the beach today,
        The size of a swollen thumb.

        On the beach today -
            Carried white sand in salted
            blue ridges.

The beach today,
    Held a secret in skeletal body.

    Beach today,
        Promised delicate rebirth.

Today
on
the
beach,

    I never found the body.

Return To Self

FALLING IN

The fall into love is no gentle slope,
It's a downhill rush,
stomach in throat.

Losing traction,
relinquishing control.
No time for park.
No place for neutral.

We balance on highs,
ignore regrets when low,

A reflection now to cast light with another,
no longer single or branded an 'other.'

BEING

The last pulse of our every breath.
    The notion that somehow through being
        present in love,
We have conquered death.

Loss seems improbable,
Loneliness ceases.
Languished laments no longer torment.

We are two as one.

FALLING OUT

Contracting abdomen, falling backwards,
Gravity fails, chaos prevails.
All magic lost, destiny gone,
Alone with fear.

Sliding grip, attention narrows,
Sadness gathers,
A mind in descent,
heart in collapse,

Take it to the bartender.

HURTING

Anger stealing breath
Fists clenched, head shaken.

Awake, asleep – no difference,
A bed, a blanket, coffee – not to be shared.

Never forgotten lust.

RETURNING

Loneliness, a fruit, refreshing in taste,
Holding fast to renewed strength.

Steps of agony,
nights quilted in tears of shame.

FORGOTTEN COFFEE

A vacant heart; this is love's fine charade.

Two as one, now undone.
A new life to own.

Take a dance class, go to church,
learn how to sing.

PART IV: FRENCH PRESS
"Longing for one last kiss!"

Hear Me, Just This Moment

David left my life; we were only twenty-three
I loved him from the moment he set eyes on me.

We met in college near the oldest dorm
He held my hand in the great October storm
that destroyed the branches of the old oak tree

that shaded us the day I lost my virginity.

I was the sorority president and he was the
football jock. We fit,
a dancing foot in a protective sock.

He graduated and moved to Europe,
correspondence through letters
and calls

to say, "I love you, how's the chronic
shoulder pain?"
How's your new job?
    I can't wait to come home
        to hold you again.

The last letter he wrote told of his
visit to Cartier jewelry,
admiring rings.
I never got another letter or a

diamond of promise.

He met a
French model with whom he would have a baby.
I think that child has a part of me.
He gave her my middle name.
I wonder if he likes her smile the

way he did
mine.

But Jake, you are my new love
You are the man I rest my head next to
You are the man I will marry
You are the man I met on the train the day
David's daughter was born.

I will think of the cracked branches of the oak tree
as we stand at the altar.

I will say, "I do," but I will mean,
"I don't."
I don't want to live without him.

Sometimes I miss him more when you are near.
I wish to say you have been my cure.
Your love only frosts my loss.

Will you hold me when I can't speak his name?
Invite my tears to dry in your chest?

Oh, my heart wilts in this constant rewind,
Why do you still want to marry me?
Why, Jake, do you remain so kind?

FORGOTTEN COFFEE

Each day you try to
love me more like I loved him,
I resist

giving you all of me.

Hear me, please –
    just this moment.

I grieve.

Ruby Heart

Gentle Stillness.
I am one with my body.

Holding onto what is left.
    Letting go of what is right.

It's bleating louder.
    The Red Gem near death
    will cauterize.

Singing His Prayer

My creased leather notebook and bound hymnal in hand,
I entered into the damp thickness of the
Coleman's cottage.

Married 71 years, Sarah and Jacob Coleman
babysat me once when I was three,
let me live with them when I was abandoned by my mom at
age five.
I should have returned to visit when they invited me.

"Sarah hasn't been to church in nearly four months.
Illness has left her mute," my pastor explained.
"Go see her. Please."

The cottage breathed its sorrows into me.
Jacob thanked me for coming.
Discomforted by its silence, I started humming a hymn.
Sarah shook, her voice, scarred from radiation
treatments, warmed in song -

At the name of Jesus every knee shall bow,
Every tongue confess Him King of glory now;

The words illness had slowly stolen, returned.

'Tis the Father's pleasure we should call Him Lord,

A voice,

Andrea Cladis

      not feeble,
      nor searching.

      A voice,
      In song for
      Jesus.

Sarah's angelic notes vibrated through Jacob's ears
bringing his discolored olive eyes to clarity
      He whistled, she sang,
light sparkled into the soft hues of her tired voice.
At His voice creation sprang at once to sight,
All the angel faces, all the hosts of light,

The pastor shared this story on Sunday.

Of how Sarah sang and Jacob Coleman came alive.

Sitting with Jacob in the half-empty pew,
    I prayed for Sarah.
    Jacob held my hand.
    His fingers delicate, his hands newly warm.
Sarah's burgundy and gold butterfly lapel graced
the left shoulder of
his stiff wool jacket.

      "Hymn #423"
    The congregation rose in unison.

Thrones and dominations, stars upon their way,
All the heavenly orders in their great array.

FORGOTTEN COFFEE

"I still love her," Jacob told me.
"Even though she can't speak my name."
His solemn hands pressed into mine.
I clasped them tightly and
readied my ears to
absorb the gift of

(Sarah's)

song.

April Robin

April robin, April robin,
    why aren't you singing?

April robin, April robin,
      why aren't you flying?

April robin, April robin,
    why are the skies so gray?

Yesterday I saw your feathers shudder
in early spring's winter winds.
Your feet like two tripods balancing on the barren earth.
Nature's missing chess piece.

April robin, April robin,
     why isn't your chest orange?

I thought dried mud covered your chest,
but yesterday's rain didn't remove
the dark stain.

April robin, April robin,
     why are you alone?

April robin, April robin,
    why is it so cold?

April robin, April robin,
     where are the others?

FORGOTTEN COFFEE

Are their chests black in mourning, too?

Oh, April robin,
Take off that ashen robe!
Sing the new spring song!
Warmth must be on its way.

Oh, April robin, please boast of the sun's orange in May!

The Mother.
The Matriarch. My Yia-Yia.

Fragile life on earth
Experiencing God's grace,
Mystery of faith.

A woman of Courage.
A woman of Honor.
A woman of Fortitude and Strength.

She has been admired by many and respected
by all those who truly knew her.
She was the sole, ubiquitous fulcrum of the Cladis family.
In a word of endearment, she's Yia-Yia,
But in terms of her life and her impact –
She's legendary.

To me, Yia-Yia meant many things, but most importantly,
Yia-Yia simply equated just one thing:

FAMILY.

When I was young I never really understood why
Family had to be number one,
But Yia-Yia was persistent in reminding
me that a strong family
was not something that you won.

FORGOTTEN COFFEE

A family was something that you work for, to
which you devote your heart and soul.
And as such, your family does not leave or abandon you,
They'll keep you grounded and in control.
Your family consists of the people who are
without question by your side,
They're an indelible stamp upon your life,
And they give you joy and pride.

No matter what the circumstance,
No matter how far you roam,
Your family are the ones who gently call you home.

Yia-Yia taught me oh, so many things – to cook,
to love to learn, but the most vital thing she taught
me is that family must remain at the center;
they're the ones for which you yearn.

Our presence was demanded – holidays, weddings, birthdays,
And now here our entire family stands
unbroken, giving JOY for her life this day.

Purple was Yia-Yia's treasured color; she cherished its royalty,
Though whenever she spoke of family,
she called for steadfast loyalty.
Renascent and creative, Yia-Yia was marked by her aplomb,
But now in striving to be like her; failure comes
and my memories leave me numb.

I told her I got another 'A' in college during
one of our beloved weekly chats,
And she said, "Of course you did, I expect
no less, you're an intelligent woman,

I've never questioned that."
"Andrea, I know you'll go places, my dear. You work
very hard just like your father and Papou and for that,
I guarantee the reward will one day come near."

When I graduated college with honors and a
4.0, there was no big congratulations from
Yia-Yia, she just modestly said, "See. I told you so."

She never allowed me to feel sorry for myself,
She'd tell me straight and she refused to let me fear:
"Believe in yourself. I know you'll be great," she said.
"You're my granddaughter and there's absolutely
nothing that a Cladis can't conquer."

I will not erase the memories.
I will not ignore the past.
Though Yia-Yia's compassion, her
dedication, her prescient ways
may slowly fade, I assure you, they will last.

When informed of Yia-Yia's passing, I was completely
bewildered and lugubrious tones overwhelmed
my ears, but now in the slow days after,
God's plan has become more clear.
For on the night she died, just before she went to sleep,
My brother, the eldest male grandchild,
knelt down to wash her feet.
He showed her that he loved her,
He demonstrated grace -
And of this I am certain, he handled her with care.

FORGOTTEN COFFEE

This image has stuck with me as tears flood my
days and nights – I see that God has blessed
our family at all times – through triumphs,
tribulations and the occasional, undue fights.

Yia-Yia's first grandchild and his wife were there,
They stopped to visit as they were passing through,
Selfless and kneeling at her feet, preparing
her with alacrity and mercy, too.

Visions of this evening have brought
a calming peace to my mind
and in such memories my faith is renewed,
for it's only God's love which defies time.

Yia-Yia's feet were sparkling as she entered Heaven's gates.
Clean, crisp and ready for the glorious eternity that awaits.

Reunited with her husband, and other family members, too.
Someday, we all shall join her, our spirits will reign anew.

Yia-Yia can never be forgotten, though it's difficult to part,
I know that I will keep her forever within my heart.

I cannot change reality.
I cannot question God's plan.
Yet through the strength of family and a fiduciary faith;
Trust in God, I can.

And so we thank God for Yia-Yia,
We thank him for her beautiful life.

Andrea Cladis

We GLORIFY His name
For in *His* time, all things are right.

In dedication to a life most resplendently lived –
One that extended far beyond our reach:

Tassie Tafilos Cladis

**ΑΙΩΝΕΙΑ ΤΗΣ Η ΜΝΗΜΗ
MAY HER MEMORY BE ETERNAL**

Love Lingers In Longing

How I long to have your hand
To hold gently in mine.

How I long to feel your mouth
The succor of your skin.

How I long to see you
Smiling back at me.

How I long to hear you say,
You are beautiful.

Your brown, brooding eyes
Your bright, floating voice
Your enchanting gaze
upon me.

How I long to laugh
How I long to tease!
Bound together, longing hearts,
linger now,
at ease.

How I long for days
when deadlines fade
as we dance to the song
you sing.

Andrea Cladis

You grasp my wrist, place my hand over the
flutter in your chest.
We pause, you hold me close.

The mountain mist of your cologne,
The strength of your castle love.

How I long for that embrace
To guard me still
My peace, my place.

Oh, how I long for one last kiss,
To be evermore warmed in love like this!

The Prince

Mining the deaths of
fallen souls.
My bestial breath

waits for each one to drop
pleading to their God
for another chance
at the fields of fragrant flowers and
ivory angels.

I love when he denies them.

I tell them the darkness heals
My dreamy eyes lure them
to the lands where their light becomes charcoal
black and sleep is never
had again.

The funeral of the soul
is my eternal beauty.

I can't wait for the next fallen hand
that reaches down only to me.

Never Just A Kiss

Like the silken wetness of
sugared iced tea
to break the humid monotony on a sticky

August day.

My face awakened to him.

Falling into his eyes,
the mint leaf from my tea

held onto my upper lip, leaving its
fusion with the cubed ice in my glass.

Cinnamon brown hair upright on his well-groomed head.
His dimples exuded a fine moxie.

I met him on a plane, not once, but three times in two years.
His teenage suave invited me to fall for his
Less-than-chivalrous charm.
I sipped sweetly tempered tea.

I was too old to be his lover,
But he wasn't too young to be mine.

His voice not quite past pubescence
carefree lyrics whistled from his
wonder-filled lips,

FORGOTTEN COFFEE

"Baby, I'm dancing in the dark with you between my arms
    Barefoot in the grass, listening to our favorite song.
When you said you looked a mess, I
whispered underneath my breath
        Darling, you look perfect tonight."

Unreachable atoms of energy within him
I wanted to settle into his
Yet unsunken chest,
Endlessly.

On my last flight to Chicago this year
I dreamt that he kissed me.

When I woke it felt like the mint leaf
was pressed against my lips,
firmly stopping my tongue,
but I found his lips were holding mine.
I pulled away.

    "It's just a kiss," he said as I hastily clutched my bags.

His smile still finds me,
His dimples I remember.

"No," I said to the lips I will not have again.
    "It's never just a *kiss*."

To Know An Angel

I woke up and asked, "How blessed am I?"
Caught my silhouette in the mirror and cried.

Shadowy, sunken,
Fallen hair.
Bruised violet circles,
Under each eye.

A tear-stained nightshirt,
The wanton desire to shout.

Minty toothpaste seared swollen gums,
A body perpetually numb.
A cluttered mind,
Imperfection whelmed.

But one grace-given angel
    Held me.

She cast aside judgment, she placed me above
Mom and Dad wanted to *fix*,
Her mission was to love.

Weariness suffocated each passing day,
The pulsing temptation to give up.

But there was this girl with a smile,
Who looked on me gently –
                  all truth, no lies.

While condescension crippled.
She'd make time to greet me,

FORGOTTEN COFFEE

She'd call me by name.

She'd tell me a story,
She'd make a silly gaffe.
Obscenely foolish, I'd stop to laugh.

Friends kept distance
But this girl, my sister, moved closer.

Was she afraid? Was she worried?
Did she see me as pure?
To help is one thing, to heal is another.
To fully sacrifice self, made certain I was no longer an "other."

She struggled inside, assuming my pain
Projecting her happiness, in bright light she came.

She followed me around; she didn't want me alone,
And to this day, she stays with me to roam.

Maybe, I'm lucky; perchance I'm blessed –
I prefer to say, I know Jesus in the flesh.

So many times she's been shaken to the core
But she gets up, she fights,
she knows her everlasting *smile* means more.

No matter the heft of the crosses she bears,
She does it with mercy; she does it with care.

A tireless example of thankless grace,
continual is her shine.

Through this angel,
I am witness to heaven.

Another Funeral

My parents go to a lot of funerals.
Yes, the Funerals.
The dinner functions.
The conferences.
The luncheons.

Funerals for peers, colleagues, relatives far past their prime.
Dinner functions of old wealth coddling
the ephemeral passage of time.
Conferences for aging adults re-financing their lives.
Luncheons for the community of retired
men and their still-lonely wives.

Mother and Father dress well; they leer
mysteriously each time they leave the house
As there are no more wedding invites nor
baby showers welcoming life.
No more brightly colored dresses, tanned skin,
flashy, coordinating pocket squares.
No more high heels, blazers, or hardened jet black hair.
No more limousine rides, alcohol on breath,
the residue of unfettered flair.

I wonder for how long they will still be mine?
For how much longer they will remember my name?
For how will I ever let go of the passing time?

These dismal events they now attend in stiffly ironed dresses,
pleated pants with room for extra weight –

FORGOTTEN COFFEE

appear to award time's passage.
Their routine attendance seems to them nary a chore.

I do not want to accept the way life takes us
one by one and two by two.

So I pray as
Mother situates her ruby broach and
Father his dated argyle tie –
    That there will always be more funerals, dinner
    functions,
        smoked salmon salad luncheons.
I pray for the polished ruby broach and the faded argyle tie,
For the day I will have to attend the
funeral and be forced to say,

Goodbye.

Unsalted Love

Laughing smoke filled Papou's lungs
as he lit another cigarette under the sticky, August sky.

His smiling eyes, inviting me to sit next to him,
exhaled.

Revealing a snack,
I held my breath next to the foggy halo of his cigarette.

I was nine-years-old.
Papou was seven, the year he started
smoking in Zakynthos, Greece -
      an island to which he would never return.

"Papou, some pretzels for you. No salt," I offered.
He took the pretzels, but angered.

His thick, welting Greek accent braced his throat.
He bellowed, "NO SALTY! NO TASTY!"

"But Papou. You're sick. Dad said too much
sodium is bad for your heart," I reminded.
"Silly ta-pramata!" He rifled back, his muffled
Greek-English version of, "Screw that!"

I giggled into the smoke cloud enveloping
the porch of his sighing home and
we ate the pretzels in silence. He hated every bite.

FORGOTTEN COFFEE

I squinted my itchy, smoke-glazed eyes
peering into Papou's shaded coke-bottle glasses.

"Papou," I said in the pocket of clean air.
"Don't you know that you're dying?"

His eyes grew wide as he patted his greasy,
thin comb-over back into place and
situated the high belted waist of his
permanently pressed gray dress pants.
He stood, wriggled, positioned his belt over the hard belly

"I may die, my kuklamou, but you, you get to
dream. Agape love dreams. You have your father,
mother, sister, brother, cousins. Fresh lamb, peace
for sleep. You're still playing and still dreaming."

His rough hands held my face; he cupped my chin.
"Be strong. You be strong. Agape love
makes you strong. And this here?
This here a good place. A very, very good place."

My small fingers etched the outline of the thin streak
of hair plastered across the top of his head.
I felt tears cooling the dryness of my eyes.
In them, the reflection of Zakynthos and Agape love.
Of gambling, card-playing immigrants who
gave up their home for a life unknown.
Of a seven-year-old boy who lit up dreams
on the butts of arid island cigarettes.
Of smoke-filled air floating above high-waisted trousers.
Of Yia-Yia's pastichio and lemon-oregano lamb.

Andrea Cladis

The mouthfeel of chalk-ready pretzels lingered in my throat.
He bent down to kiss me.
I bristled from the smoky, discomforting touch.

But I still wanted him to kiss me again so
I opened my lungs to take in the smoky air of his love.

Farewell

He latched the weary gates behind him.
White shutters and brick stone
watched his agony.

The cloudy windows stared.
The front room like an empty casket
mocking the fragile lives he took.

The doorway stoop a vacant nest.
    A place unfit for new dreams.

Inside the home a faded portrait smiled
from the dusty marble coffee table.
    His mother, his father, frozen in matrimony
        They had just met on their wedding day.

From Zakynthos to America
Speaking in native tongue
With eager eyes of zest for wealth in
    A land far from home.

Years of lost relatives who could not immigrate
Years of gambling away money that was to support a family
    The peeling, pale rose wallpaper
        Shouted in whispered echoes of argument and hubris.

A Greek flag with fraying edges
waved slowly above their son who stood

helpless in the shadow of white and blue,
Bewildered in anguish.

The White Sox hat on his head - the ballcap of his youth
The unkempt lawn where his father taught him to play
The all-American sport that became his passion day after day.

The chimney sighed the hollow smoke
of his father's final cigarette
The Grecian flowerpots rested their monumental grief
The perpetual radio chattered on telling
their son the world goes on
And the weather update on the 8's
insistent on more clouds and rain.

Following the crippled sidewalk path to the street,
he squeezed his fists; he cried.
The boy who played here now a man
Kneeled on the patched dirt grass as
his head sunk past his knees.

He could see the sandlot baseball games
He smelled the lemon oregano lamb
roasting on the greasy spit in
He heard the Greek chants of anise libation

He watched his father grow ill of the chimney's smoke
and his mother's guilt-riddled ways mature to silence,
fade into the black she wore after her husband's passing.
The erosion of her sharp, matriarchal vitality.

The crumbling sidewalk cracks pulsed at his retreat.

FORGOTTEN COFFEE

And the driveway he re-surfaced every year
refused to lead him to the street.
      where the empty Lincoln Mercury sat on the curb
          near the mailbox hunched over by the weight of
          unread, purple letters
addressed to her prized sons and grandchildren.

The radio clamoured the scores of the game,
The humid air was being greedy,
      stealing spaces between his childhood and his chest.

He unsealed the lavender scented letter addressed to him
and buried it carefully alongside his cap next to the mailbox
where it would remain hidden by the earth's protection.

The house sighed in taunt of his action
and quietly wept.

The burdened brick stone,
No longer a home,
ached without
a sentient soul.

About the Author

Andrea Cladis holds an MFA in Writing from Fairfield University and is a Summa Cum Laude graduate of Elmhurst College with degrees in English Writing, Interdisciplinary Communications, French, and Secondary Education. A former journalist and High School English teacher, she currently works as a college English professor, freelance editor, writing consultant, and fitness professional. She has worked for Delnor Hospital's Marketing and Public Relations Department, for neighborhood magazines, and as a feature writer for Shaw Media. She has been published by *SAGE Academic*, *The Greek Star*, various literary journals, and online publications including Thought Catalog, Elite Daily, and Patch.com. She is the author of the memoir, *Tatsimou, Hold On* (Adelaide Books, 2018), and the Christian nonfiction book, *Finding the Finish Line: Navigating the Race of Life through Faith & Fitness* (CrossLink Publishing, 2017). She has written extensively for online news websites, print magazines, local newspapers, and social media blogs. Known for her sharp observations and sense of humor, Andrea's writing has been described as "emotive, yet brazen, seasoned with thinly veiled cynicism, and a pinch of sarcasm." Andrea is an Advisory Board Member for Cambridge Scholars Publishing and maintains a personal site about faith, fitness, writing, and public speaking engagements which can be explored at www.andreacladis.com.

Acknowledgments

A special thank you to the faculty and staff at Fairfield University who have formatively shaped my vision as a poet-artist. To Karen Osborn, for your wit, patience, and keen sense of perception in guiding me towards poets of like mind. To Da Chen, for encouraging me to pursue nonfiction writing and a memoir project. Had it not been for your insight, guidance, and genuine care for me and my personal story, I never would have had the courage to write and to publish. To Baron Wormser, for counsel in the art of spiritual writing, for teaching me distinct ways to enter into the life of a poem and to embody the experience of creation. Baron, for your continued poetic wisdom in helping me to learn the value of word economy and to appreciate the careful construction of a poem's soundscape. To Sonya Huber, for your enthusiasm for storytelling and pursuit of excellence in the written word, I thank you. And to the men and women of Ender's Island who graciously allow Fairfield University students to submerse themselves in art while on the most peaceful isle that led to the production of much of this poetry, I thank you.

To my parents, Jane and Peter Cladis, for educating me from a young age to take a vested interest in learning about the people and things that compose the world around me. From being an editor of my long essays or research projects, to reading my writing and taking a genuine interest in my art. For your ready critique to push me past the comfortable bias of my personal perspective, and for your steadfast attitude in support of me through my continued journey as an artist. I love you for loving me, never giving up on me, and for being the solid pillars that have formed the foundation of my life.

To my grandparents who patiently listened to me tell countless stories when I was young and who always told me to follow the tether that God had placed on my heart. I will use my writing to keep your memory eternal.

To my siblings, Dennis and Stacey, who willingly accept and love me as the quirky middle child, and who have provided me with a plethora of cherished childhood memories which still inform my writing. Thank you for being the best brother and sister an artist could ask for.

To my husband, Matthew, for shunning unfavorable societal views of artists and encouraging me to devote myself to that which fuels my soul. For sitting next to me during long writing sessions, your presence was my security in the unknown. For learning to write poetry only because you knew it would resonate with my heart. For holding my hand and forcing me to stop long enough to absorb the hidden beauty of this world. For your imagination and humor that nourish my curiosity. And finally, for believing that no matter what comes of the creative works I produce, I am always a success in your eyes.

Lastly, I thank my Father in Heaven for the miraculous gift of living in this world and sharing in His abundant creation. May the words I write forever glorify Him. For as an artist in the world, it is my mission to be a lighthouse for the lost, a refuge for the broken, a leader of progress, a catalyst for critical thinking, and most importantly, an interminable agent for the beauty of imagination.

www.ingramcontent.com/pod-product-compliance
Lightning Source LLC
Chambersburg PA
CBHW032231080426
42735CB00008B/806